LIFE IS FULL OF Inspiration!

Poetry to refresh the soul...

Y. K. M. SYMONETTE

Copyrights

ISBN 9798332948411

Inspire Publishing (Bahamas)

www.InspirePublishing.org

Author Contact:

Y. K. M. Symonette

P. O. Box N-1135

Nassau, Bahamas

Telephone: (242) 431-5487

Email: sym17178@gmail.com

Acknowledgements

I thank the true and living God for giving me a desire to write and for then furnishing the words! I thank the family and friends that made me stretch in contemplation of our relationships, which made me put pen to paper, and write of those feelings.

I thank the Ministry of Education and its Evaluation Department that scrutinized this book and subsequently deemed it appropriate for use in our school system.

I thank the wonderful management and staff of the National Library of the Bahamas for cataloguing this booklet.

I thank the many friends and associates, who after reading the first production, gave their impressions, opinions, and encouragement of this work.

Dedication

Without reservation, I dedicate this book to the two beings who have most inspired me—my heavenly Father and my earthly father!

Introduction

This collection of poems was written over a few years, with each poem being designed as individual inspirational pieces to display on posters, cards, and even for a newsletter.

Unwittingly, I realized that this collection had culminated into a poetry book that would appeal to a full spectrum of readers.

While deciding on the arrangement of this group of poems, I must concede there is a certain amount of magnetism—in their simplicity and underlying inspirational connotation.

I am humbled and honored to have produced such works. I hope you find it as satisfying and enjoyable a work as I do.

These are all examples of how—

“Life Is Full of Inspiration!”

Table of Contents

Poems of the Butterfly

The Butterfly

It swoops, hovers, flits, and flies,
A pretty butterfly,
Looping from here to there,
Only God knows where.

Floating and meandering along without fear,
Seemingly without the least bit of care,
Stopping to taste this or that flower,
Functioning on natural power.

Over the water, over the land,
Testing its wings—fulfilling the plan,
You see a pretty butterfly,
He knows this creature must flow in His supply,
You see this creature as a display,
Or something that lives to play.

He knows the butterfly must go as it goes,
It carries life flows,
You see, it distributes pollen from flower to flower,
It brings with it, but it also takes with it life power.

Butterfly is symbolic of life, you know,
Don't its actions show?
Metamorphosis is also synonymous with its name,
For from a caterpillar to a butterfly—it became,
Never again to be the same.

The Butterfly in You

The power to become is within you,
The power to change is within you,
The power to live life is within you,
Choice activates these powers.

The power to be affected and to affect is within you,
The power to feel rejected and to reject—is within you,
You must choose it!

There is a butterfly in all of us,
Its wings are beating in waves of life,
Can't you feel the spasms echoing throughout your entire being?

Yes, its speaking to you,
Attempting to empower you from the inside out,
Life is shouting—
"Let me infect you—let me change you!"
Let me live out life in you.

"Life"—the ultimate life is the "Giver of Life"!
Let life live in you—
Answer the beat of the butterfly in you!

Poems of the Sea

The Sea

Tumultuous its waves, as it reaches onto the earth,
Its boundary skirting land and sky,
It roars, rages, pants, puffs, and stands still . . .
It enters and exits, taking with it and leaving evidence of its presence—at its will.

Forms, shapes, expands—exclusive or vague—footprints,
Can't you see it?
There it goes and comes, already here, gone nowhere,
It has existed from time began.

Its depths are still mysterious, lurking with creatures we can't conceive,
You would have to have existed, as long as it has, for you to believe.

Its power seems almost mystical yet it's submissive,
Anything can gain entrance to it wherever it flows,
But not everything that gains entrance can go where it goes.

It's therapeutic, it evokes passion, it's medicinal,
It's soothing, it's recreational,
It can be called home to some, a financial gain,

A calming release to emotional pain.

It contains food and life, it's a cleansing power,
It guides us by its ebbs and flows—by the hour.
It's a wonder something so passive yet powerful, can be so contained,
But yes, one mightier spoke and it became.
Then He set its boundaries saying, "So far, no further."
He spoke and it ran to its place,
He who fashioned it and commanded it, gave it to this human race.

Catch of the Day

They get out before the break of day,
They're on a mission—to a secret hiding spot,
It's not plotted on any map, but they know the way,
To find the most succulent fish, to go in our pot.

So, when you come you better realize,
Every catch taken is fresh—that's placed before your eyes.

From right out of the boat and into the pan,
Cooked to delight you, as best we can.
So, we ask that you come, enjoy, and gladly pay,
For our scrumptious "catch of the day"!

Ocean Seen?

It isn't blue,
It isn't green,
Or turquoise,
Or aquamarine,

Though, what is its true sheen?
Is it what's realistically seen?
Sometimes it appears to be blackest of blue,
But is that its truest hue?

What if I told you, this body of water is devoid of colour?
That from this perplexing mystery you will discover,

The ocean gets its pigmentation,
From elements of depth and light reflection,
And the diversity of its flora population.

Haven't you ever attempted to save some of its marvellous colour for yourself?
So, you could have a portion of it, to gaze at its beauty on a shelf?

But with poignant dismay you find,
Somehow, that delectably elusive hue got left behind!

Poems of Advice

Know When to Say "No"

You must know when to say "NO,"
No matter where you go,
Who you're with, what you're saying or doing,
There comes a time when the only applicable word is—
"NO."

"No" is universal,
It is the shortest dismissal,
"No" crosses language barriers,
There's "no" mix-ups, "no" needs, "no" priors.

"No" can be said by young or old,
If on something you're not sold,
You don't have to fold,
Let them be easily told!

Say "NO" without feeling ashamed,
Say "NO" without any refrain,
Say "NO," it could save you a whole lot of pain,
Saying "NO" may even keep you sane.

It was a good reason vocabulary was affected by adding "NO,"
It was no mistake that word "NO" was created,

It's quite easy to say,
Just open your mouth, and form those two letters and you're on your way.

Remember, no means no, there's no denying,
"No" cuts short chances of lying,
Saying "no" may mean the difference between living or dying.

So, when you're not certain about which way to go,
Sometimes, it just takes you knowing, when to say—
"NO!"

Customer Service

Annie-Mae was on der phone wid her peeps,
When der other phone line beeps,
She switched to the customer on line two,
And told them, in a huff: "Hol' on, I'll get back to you!"
Then many minutes "on hold," after no further reply,
The customer hung up and drove by.

Annie-Mae still on der phone talkin' to her cous',
Heard the doorbell buzz,
"Naw, who could dat be?!"
"Well, I busy, so, dey better wait on me!"

After a while the customer went away,
That was the only customer who came by that day,
You think this affected Annie-Mae's pay?
I'd say!

People take heed to this lesson,
The customer is your blessing,
On customer service—
Let me give you some advice,
To your customers be receptive, courteous, and nice.

Think. Think. Think …

Think love, not hate,
Think positive, know when to wait,
Think joy and there'll be no space for pain,
Think true fellowship and we'll think less of casting blame,

Think peace,
You'll experience God's release,
Think good thoughts,
As you ought,
Thinking this way will set you free,
And free, is how your Creator wants you to be!

Ever Get Tired?

Ever felt so tired you thought you might . . .
Give up the fight?
You know, these fights we all MUST go through,
These fights that make you evolve into you,
These fights we know we're in,
But sometimes we think we may not win.

Doesn't it feel like this is some kind of roller-coaster ride?
One you feel you can't abide.
From which, you try to run and hide?
And then there's no one there in whom you can confide,
Someone who you can tell it all to and leave the burden behind!

Hey, STOP! . . . before you go all the way down that road,
The one that causes you to think dreary, melancholy thoughts and brood,
That gets you in a dreadful, stinky mood.

Say this: "I know Your Spirit in me, makes me cherished,
Not perished,"
Hear that?
Your Creator's telling your truth, not fact,
That He made you,

So wonderfully and awesomely too.

He put you together to serve a purpose—right here on Earth,
Your life has much worth,
Even though He formed your predecessor from the dirt,
So, when you get tired and feeling down,
Remember, it's God who's keeping you alive and around!

Give Thanks!

For helpful hands willing to serve,
For patient words that calm the nerve,
For simple everyday tasks,
For treasured memories that last,

For a job that pays the rent,
For time already spent,
For past, present and times to come,
For what you are now and even what you could become,

For a roof overhead and something to eat,
For a little left over to give yourself a treat,
For family and friends,
For God's saving grace and helping hands,
For these are the things that will matter when your lifetime ends.

Poems of Relationship

Love Is ...

A kind word,
A helpful hand,
A well-meant gesture,
These are things that should give pleasure,
And show love's measure.

The cry of a new-born babe,
The beginning of a brand-new day,
Newlyweds consummating their union,
In all-engulfing passion,
Life-giving devotion.

Sacrifice and giving,
Family getting along,
Even when folk do wrong,
Seeing them in a good light with sensitivity,
Covering loved ones, in the spirit of loyalty.

A decision . . .
Responding to a plea,
Putting yourself in someone else's shoe,
Having vision to affect more than just you,
Not adding to a mess,

The certainty of trust,
Seeking to do what's right and just,
Love is . . . God!

Father

F—a faithful and stable foundation,

A—He earns his family's admiration,

T— A man true to his word, prepared to go above and beyond,

H—To honour his bond,

E—He endures life's hardships to keep his family secure,

R—He is a real provider,

He is a father.

Mother

M—A motivator and humble mentor,

O—She guides her folk as a vigilant overseer,

T—Always prepared to instruct, advise, or discipline, is this teacher,

H—Harmony flows in her veins, she is an accomplished homemaker,

E—Excellence is her living, she is a life example,

R—She is a relevant nurturer,

She is a mother.

Marriage

It's not just a fancy ceremony or a lease for sexual bliss,
It's not just started at the altar with the "I Do's" and a kiss,
It's far more than just all this,
So don't enter it, with thoughts amiss.

It's seeing yourself with that person forever,
A life-long endeavour,
It's knowing that person is your friend, your comrade, your mate,
With that one, you should find it a joy to relate,
You should honour them with your love and patience,
This love affair should have much resilience.

After all, didn't you say . . .
You know, on that big day,
That your love is here to stay?
So, what on this earth could possibly make that go away!

It's being satisfied with your acts in privacy,
And blessed with the fruit of your intimacy,
Yes, those dear children, the semblance of the both of you,
Adding to your lives, becoming the focus of the things you now do,
Now, there's just more of you to secure, love, and bring through.

But. Let's go deeper,
For marriage has a holy keeper,
He saw the first marriage done,
When Adam looked on Eve and said, "You're the one."
The Lord said when a man finds a wife, he finds a good thing,
He'll leave father and mother and to his wife he would cling.

He said to the man: "Husband, love your wife,
For her, you must be prepared to give your life."
He said to the woman: "Wife, to your husband submit,
And in good conduct, he will to you, his life commit."
Then He commanded them both: "In love you must exist and be,
And your union would always be blessed by Me."

Vessel of Honour

In the middle of romantic fascination,
Did you focus on your pre-destination?
Then while you were saying: "I Do,"
Did you know it would be you?

When you shared rapture on that sacred bed,
Did you have any thought of me in your head?
Well, while I was in that precious state of pause,
So unaware that I was made for a cause,
The Creator knew the exact moment when,
He would place me into a womb open.

He had planned me from the beginning, you see,
How I would look, walk, talk—everything that would make me, me.
He who is the Beginning and the End—chose you.
To plant me in, then to bring me through,
He gave you strength to endure the labour,
That's why you are called a "*Vessel of Honour*."

The Greatest Dad on Earth!

We just had to tell you—thank you, Dad!
Thanks for being there,
And proving to us how much you really care!
Thanks for hearing ALL our problems too,
Thanks for your advice that directed us in what we should do,
For we know it was never your course,
To try to live our lives for us or to be our boss.
No, you knew for us to come through,
You would have to train us how to do the things we would need to do.
How to say what was on our mind,
Yet how to be nice, to be kind.

Dad, thank you for being a tower of strength,
To go the distance—width and length,
To bring us through.
And even when it seemed that we didn't get the picture,
You would go back over it and throw some more wisdom in the mixture!

Thank you, Dad, when today it seemed that the latest fashion,
Was a dad, running out on his kids and showing NO compassion,
But in this was not your way,

For you determined, you would be there for your children—come what may!
Even when in our house things were amiss,
You didn't check for that thing or this,
You didn't give up, you didn't lose hope,
You pulled us through as if with an imaginary rope.

Thank you, Dad, for letting us live our lives through,
Without trying to make us into a carbon copy of you,
For letting us become the people we were destined to be,
Functioning, dreaming, excelling and being free,
For letting us learn by our own mistakes,
After all, isn't that what it takes?
There's so much more we can thank you for, Dad,
For it's been your life's worth,
That's why we've elected you *the Greatest DAD on Earth!*

My Big Bro

When you're the oldest, folk expect you'll automatically be strong,
That you can't do and go much wrong,
But do they take into consideration that you're human too?
That you'll have to learn out of the good, yes,
And the silliness that you'll do?
Since when is a person perfect?
Only one walked this earth, died, and resurrected,
And only He deserves that title of respect.

Though sometimes . . . you feel you got something to prove,
Move by move,
Hey, big bro', ease up and you'll see,
It takes more than living and controlling to be free!
It takes a special kind of man to cry,
A man that doesn't have to know all the reasons why,
That one that knows he is not insignificant,
That one that isn't driven by lust for things or power to prove that he's important.

Don't let anything or anyone make you stray,
Cause that's not the true intended way,
Bro', I had to learn to deal with the past too man,
I had to learn to accept that all of us only human,

Bound to make mistakes,
Bound to try and go our own way, no matter what it takes,
Then one day—and it's bound to happen—we come to some sense,
And realize—without the real dose of truth—what utter nonsense!

Hey, I'm not preaching,
Or trying to influence whatever conclusion you'll be reaching,
I just want you to know:
"Whatever you do, and no matter wherever you go,
You'll always be my big bro'!"

No One

No one can feel my pain,
No one to hurt me again,
No one to hear me cry,
No one to say "Goodbye,"
No one to come home to,
No one there when I'm sad and blue,
No one, no, no one, until I met You.

No one to share a joke,
No one to lovingly stroke,
No one to join hands with in hope,
No one to throw me a saving rope,
No one to cherish,
No one who cares if I perish,
No one knew I was shaking up,
No one, no, no one, until You showed up.

No one really thought of me,
No one was who they thought I would be,
No one, no, no one, could picture the me, I now see,
No one, no, no one, knew, the me, You, created me to be!

I Miss You!

Your muffled tones,
The slightest suggestion of your smile,
Your mischievous glance,
Your earnest candour,
Your presence,
Your face . . .

The way you call my name,
I can see, I'm important in your eyes,
When we're together, everyone else disappears,
Love soars, there is no fear,

Our love is . . .
Pure and innocent in action,
Strong in purpose,
Faithful in union,
Predestined.

I miss you . . .
And I know with every part of my being—instinctively—that,
. . . you miss me too!

Poems of Expectation

The Gift

I was asked to sit and close my eyes,
I was about to get a surprise,
Then he placed something on my lap, that I was told to navigate—
eyes closed—my gift I would realize.

The first layer was of usual shape—rectangular, wrapped and
with a bow,
I ripped away the wrapping and lid, feeling my way around now,
But to my dismay, I felt another box inside,
My hand flew out, trying to find him—to pinch, poke or hit—this
joke I couldn't abide.

He insisted I go on—
"Oh, and keep your eyes closed," he said,
I thought—
Was there something about this matter that I should dread?

I continued, feeling a little foolish for listening,
For it seemed, with this gift, something was missing,
My hand connected with the second lid,
I tore it off to feel inside and to find what was hid,
Under some paper I found the item,
What was it? Hard, cold, designed in some way,

Shaped like a circle with a trim?
I gave up and turned the game over to him.

He said, "This gift is for you, but it also can serve me,
Open your eyes and you'll see."
I did, and found myself looking into an ornate, gold-toned, oval shaped mirror,
While I sat, admiring the craftsmanship of the mirror's manufacturer,
He sat cherishing the reflected image, crafted by the Creator.

A New Thing

Can't you see it springing forth?
With your old, unchanged eyes you won't see it as you ought,

Look—See—Focus!
Discern, listen, don't discuss,
Once you cried out for help and it seemed pointless,
Now help is here and measureless.

People would want to know, where this new thing in you was found,
Now good health and much wealth abound,
Tell them and be real,
Don't worry how they will feel,

And stay away from their clichés, that's only a swing,
They only want to claim some of your bling,
Let them know, the One who created everything out of nothing,
Is deserving full credit for this new thing!

Independence

We begin our lives so totally dependent,
So vulnerable and small,
Oblivious to how to live life at all,

Then comes the choices:
Learn how to creep, then stand tall,
Even if sometimes you'd fall,
Learn your lessons good,
You'll need them in the world to be understood,
Learn how to drive,
It's a quick and easy way to arrive,
Learn how to earn your pay,
You'll become a success one day,
Learn how to treat people with regard,
Put yourself in their shoes, and it won't be hard,
Learn the truest path to your next generation,
Is marriage first, then reproduction,

But our greatest declaration of independence is from a sinful fall,
When we heard and responded to that clarion call,
And made the best independent choice of all.

A Wish

Is it real? Or akin to hope?
Is it like writing a promissory note?

Is it magical?
I hear folk wish for this or that,
As if they were pulling tricks out of a hat!

If you had one wish,
Something, anything that you could do,
What would you wish?
What would you want to have come true?

Departure

When we leave . . .
Collapse, depart, exit this mortal plain,
Out of chaos, comes relief,
Out of pain and sorrow,
Comes peace,
Out of constant cares for tomorrow,
Comes a sweet release,

When we leave . . .
Family and friends and acquaintances too,
See you from alternating points of view,
To those who knew you in joy and laughter,
Your loss is a disaster . . .
A few may discover remorse,
And give silent pause,
Those who procrastinated and spent little time with you, will regret,
All the lost opportunities, and may fret . . .
Others with hope in their heart,
Tearfully accept the inevitable depart,
The ones we leave behind in faith and love,
Will expect to unite with us, above . . .

Don't become so enthralled by living,
And not recognize, every day is dying,
You brought nothing when you came, and taking nothing when you go,
No bags to pack, no baggage to stow,
Examine where you fit in the departure zone,
Because man or woman, young or old, rich or poor, black or white,
Departure may be coming soon . . .

Resurrection

His blood shed for mercy's sake,
His blood was what judgment would take,
His blood paid the price,
His blood was love's sacrifice,
His blood pure and unblemished,
His blood spoke, and then it was finished.

His blood gained our salvation,
His blood brings us to the Father without reservation,
In His blood we can trust,
His blood keeps us fortified and robust.

His blood washed away sin's power and insurrection,
His blood brought clarity and correction,
His blood was God's prophesied re-connection,
His blood seals our eternal selection,
His blood, ever-living, is the proof of the resurrection!

Life Is Full of Inspiration

This book's author was inspired to put pen to paper on many occasions to send some lasting, heart-felt words to a few families and friends.

While these words may have been written at those times for that handful of individuals, the author realized these writings would also apply to a wider audience. Thus, this collection of poems was published.

It is hoped that you discover literary keepsakes here that will impact situations in your life and evoke repetitive reading of this book!

One More Thing

Thank you for taking the time to read Life Is Full of Inspiration! Your decision to secure a copy of this book is truly appreciated. I would be honored to receive your feedback. If you purchased your copy on Amazon.com, it would be a great help if you could leave an honest review of the book. If you received it as a gift or purchased it locally, please drop me a line with your thoughts. Reviews are immensely valuable to authors as they help more people discover our books and share the good news. Thank you once again, and I look forward to hearing from you soon!

Yvette K. M. Symonette